Healthy Living

Sleep

by Vanessa Black

Ideas for Parents and Teachers

Bullfrog Books let children practice reading informational text at the earliest reading levels. Repetition, familiar words, and photo labels support early readers.

Before Reading

- Discuss the cover photo. What does it tell them?
- Look at the picture glossary together. Read and discuss the words.

Read the Book

- "Walk" through the book and look at the photos. Let the child ask questions. Point out the photo labels.
- Read the book to the child, or have him or her read independently.

After Reading

- Prompt the child to think more. Ask: How much sleep do you think you get a night? How do you feel about going to bed? How about waking up?

Bullfrog Books are published by Jump!
5357 Penn Avenue South
Minneapolis, MN 55419
www.jumplibrary.com

Library of Congress Cataloging-in-Publication Data

Names: Black, Vanessa, author.
Title: Sleep / by Vanessa Black.
Description: Minneapolis, MN: Jump!, Inc. [2017]
Series: Healthy living | "Bullfrog Books are published by Jump!." | Audience: Ages 5–8.
Audience: K to grade 3.
Includes bibliographical references and index.
Identifiers: LCCN 2016029370
ISBN 9781620315477 (hardcover: alk. paper)
ISBN 9781620315842 (pbk.)
ISBN 9781624964954 (ebook)
Subjects: LCSH: Sleep—Juvenile literature.
Health—Juvenile literature.
Classification: LCC RA786 .B53 2017
DDC 613.7/94—dc23
LC record available at https://lccn.loc.gov/2016029370

Editor: Jenny Fretland VanVoorst
Book Designer: Molly Ballanger
Photo Researcher: Molly Ballanger

Photo Credits: All photos by Shutterstock except: Getty, 20–21, 23tl; Thinkstock, 10–11, 23bl.

Printed in the United States of America at Corporate Graphics in North Mankato, Minnesota.

Table of Contents

Sweet Dreams!

Sam is tired. What should she do?

She goes to bed.

She turns off the lights.

She sleeps.

Good sleep is important.

It helps every part of you.

Sleep helps you solve problems.

Kira is rested.

She is ready for her math test.

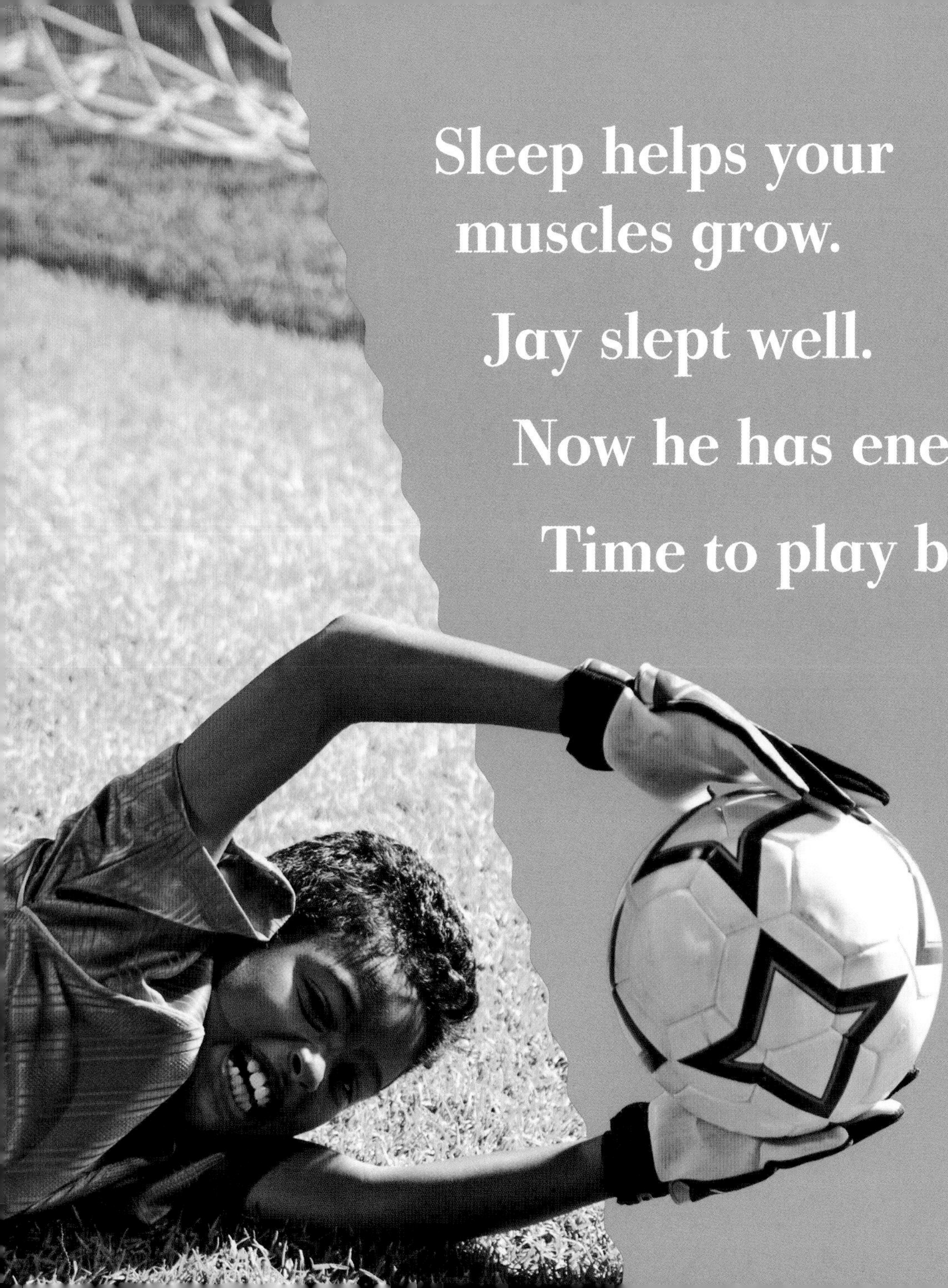

Sleep helps your muscles grow.

Jay slept well.

Now he has energy.

Time to play ball!

Sleep helps you be happy.

Lee was cranky.

She took a nap.

Now she feels better.

She smiles.

She is kind to her friends.

Sleep helps you fight sickness.

Luc has a cold.

He gets extra sleep.
Soon he is better.

Sleep helps your brain.

It helps your body.

It helps you be your best self.

Sweet dreams!

A Good Night's Sleep

Here are some things you can do to make sure you get a good night's sleep:

bedtime
Go to bed around the same time every night. Get 10 to 11 hours of sleep every night.

room
Make your room as quiet and dark as possible.

drinks
Do not have drinks with caffeine (coffee, tea, soda) within several hours of bedtime. Make sure you drink enough water during the day.

electronics
Do not watch TV or use electronic devices at least one hour before bed; read instead.

exercise
Getting at least 60 minutes of exercise every day will help you sleep better.

Picture Glossary

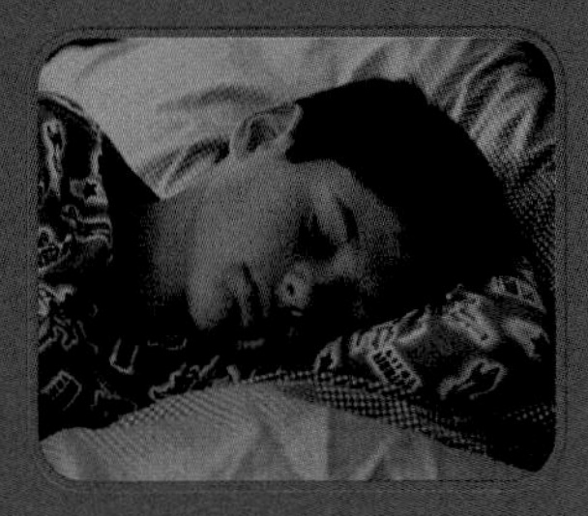

dreams
Thoughts, feelings, and images that you think about while you are sleeping.

rested
Having had enough sleep to function well.

muscles
The tissues in your body that help you move.

solve problems
To be able to think of ideas or answers for something.

Index

To Learn More

Learning more is as easy as 1, 2, 3.

1) Go to www.factsurfer.com

2) Enter "sleep" into the search box.

3) Click the "Surf" button to see a list of websites.

With factsurfer.com, finding more information is just a click away.